Lynyrd Skynyrd, Ronnie Van Zant and Me...Gene Odom

Scott Coner

iUniverse, Inc.
Bloomington

Lynyrd Skynyrd, Ronnie Van Zant, and Me ... Gene Odom

iUniverse books may be ordered through booksellers or by contacting:

iUniverse
1663 Liberty Drive
Bloomington, IN 47403
www.iuniverse.com
1-800-Authors (1-800-288-4677)

ISBN: 978-1-4620-0695-3 (sc)
ISBN: 978-1-4620-0697-7 (ebook)
ISBN: 978-1-4620-0696-0 (dj)

Library of Congress Control Number: 2011905263

Printed in the United States of America

iUniverse rev. date: 4/15/2011

Prologue

REALLY DIDN'T KNOW HOW I was going to get this whole thing started. I have read hundreds of books, but I have never considered trying to write one. But, what the heck? Maybe I can actually pull this thing off. I mean, I've been a Skynyrd fan since I was about 15 years old. I have often wondered how I've gone so many years without growing tired of their music, but somehow, it has become ingrained into my mind and soul. This book matters to me. Gene Odom matters to me. Maybe, if I'm lucky, it will speak to you as well. I am about to tell you a story about one of the nicest men I have ever met, and he is one of my closest friends. He was one of Ronnie's closest friends, he was on the plane, and that was really just the beginning…

Gene Odom was born and raised on the west side of Jacksonville, Florida. His boyhood was a simple one. He was from a large, poor family. Baseball, football, fishing, and moon pies- kind of puts the whole thing in perspective. Close your eyes for a second and drift off to a more innocent time in America. Toughskin blue jeans, plaid button down cotton shirts, flat-top haircuts, bicycles, and neighbors that still cared about the neighborhood and all who lived in it. You know, that is what makes Gene Odom special. He is an unapologetic product of the south and part of what makes our country great.

Before we get all up into this tale, let me ask you a question or two. Do you have any true friends? The kind of friend that you are there for when things get really tough? Have you ever been completely committed to someone only to see the whole thing fall apart? Have you ever looked over the edge of sanity and wondered if you can make it back to something close to clarity? I have, and that is why I wanted to write this book. Go get something cold to drink and you and me will get started. I know that we don't know each other yet, but we will. We're really all the same anyway…or are we?

Chapter 1
1974

"If You want to talk Fishin; That'll be okay."

THE PHONE STARTED RINGING WHILE it was still dark. He looked over at the alarm clock and crawled out of the perfectly warm bed. As he answered the kitchen phone, the voice on the other end said, "Are you ready to go yet?" He smiled a sleepy smile. His buddy, Ronnie Van Zant was ready to go fishing. Gene looked out the window over the sink. The street lights allowed him to see that the wind was calm and the car hoods were dry up and down the street. He grabbed a bottle of RC cola out of the refrigerator and went back to the bedroom closet to put on some jeans and a tee shirt as quietly as possible. He didn't want to wake his wife, Brenda Joe, and little Melissa. He grabbed his wallet, kissed his wife on the cheek, and headed out to the car port to gather his fishing gear. He could hear the truck coming up Mull Street as he picked up his tackle box. He nearly dropped everything as he turned to leave the garage. Maybe later today would be a good time to talk to Melissa about how to use the kickstand on her bike.

The truck stopped in the middle of the street. Gene opened the truck door to be greeted by a long haired rock 'n' roll star that was

1

truly glad to see him. "How's it going Buddy?" The radio was playing "Silver Wings," and Merle Haggard sounded like he meant every word. As the truck ambled slowly around the corner, it was just like it had always been. Two young men from the same neighborhood, the same school, the same world. Yet the dreams were different. Life can sure throw some curve balls.

It seemed like yesterday that these same men were just teenagers, barely 15 years old, "jukin' "at some neighborhood party, trying to act cool, hoping to meet a girl. Any girl..."How is life on the road? You know you're gettin' pretty well known for tearing up hotels. Doesn't that hurt the bottom line just a little bit?" Ronnie looked a little bit embarrassed. "Man, those hotels are like being put into some kind of prison. We spend day and night together and sometimes you just want to blow off a little steam, you know? The music is all that matters anyway. And maybe bad press is better than no press." Gene just laughed and said, "You are gettin' press, there ain't no doubt about it. I'll tell you one thing, when this music thing slows down, if it ever does, we ought to get you into politics. You know people hear what you're saying in those songs. We could get you to be governor and maybe I could be like a fishing ambassador or something."

The water was slick as glass when they dropped the boat in. There was a sliver of pink showing in the eastern sky. It was going to be hot, but not until later in the day. Right now, all things seemed perfectly aligned to catch a fish.

"I stopped by Claude Hamner's midway grocery store yesterday. That "Curtis Loew" song has really put some smiles on some faces around here. I'm not really used to hearing Skynyrd when I'm buying bologna for my lunch at work." Ronnie laughed and said, "I can't believe all of this is happening myself. Me and Gary and Allen were talking about it the other day during sound check. It seems like yesterday we were running around the block, throwing rocks and sneakin' cigarettes.

A mullet jumped out of the water making a splash 50 feet from the boat. "You know I can feel that bass swimming our way right now. One of us is going to catch a monster."

Ceremoniously, the water broke across the top as Ronnie's pole nearly fell out of his grip. "Gene! I've got something on the other end of this thing!" It truly was a trophy and Gene had never seen his friend happier. It was May 1977.

The following poem was written by a young Gene Odom not too long after the Lynyrd Skynyrd plane crash. He had apparently started writing as a type of self- induced therapy. This poem and several others appeared in a book written by Gene titled "Lynyrd Skynyrd I'll Never Forget You". (Ten thousand copies were made and self- published by Gene. While traveling with the groups The Rossington Collins Band, The Allen Collins Band, and finally Molly Hatchet, Gene sold the books after the shows)

The Phone Call

The bird still flies around my home
The fish still hangs on the wall
That old truck still runs the same
And I'm just waiting on your call
Those 4:30 calls we used to make
To wake each other up
Are not forgotten to this day
And probably never will be
The poles are now gathered with dust
The boat sits idle and free
Fishing trips I take these days
are not what they used to be
I lay and stare at the phone
and wait for it to ring
All of a sudden I remember
I'm only in a dream

Chapter 2
1948-1969

"Tuesdays Gone with the Wind and Tomorrow doesn't look much better"

GENE ODOM WAS BORN IN December 1948 at Duvall Medical Center. Life was pretty good. Ansal and Annie Odom were apparently committed to repopulating the earth. Gene had four brothers and six sisters. A typical day in the neighborhood consisted of playing football in the old church lot across from Claude's Midway Grocery store, cutting grass at home or for someone down the street, or just doing what kids did in 1950s America. Life was still new and innocent and lately, that seems pretty refreshing.

When Gene was 17, he and a friend, Harold Osteen, went jukin' on a Friday night at the National Guard Armory on Wilson Boulevard on the west side of Jacksonville. Gene, being the outgoing personality that he is, didn't need but a couple of cups of grape kool-aid to get out on the dance floor. When Gene busts a move, it is always the "west side shuffle". (That was always and still is his dance.) He asked a pretty little brunette to dance, and she must have had some great moves of her own because Gene asked her out the next night, and the night after that. They would go to the movies, go dancing, and sometimes just go for a walk. Although Gene had quit school and started working as an iron worker, Brenda was still in school. She was 16 and Gene was a 17- year- old man of the world. Brenda's father worked for the Florida Parks Service and took a job opportunity near Pensacola. Brenda's family relocated to the Florida Caverns State Park, about 250 miles west of Jacksonville. That was a very sad day for both Gene and Brenda. After about a month of letters and a few phone calls, Gene talked a friend of his into a road trip over to Pensacola, Florida. When Brenda and Gene reunited they realized that they truly were in love. Gene asked Brenda to come back to Jacksonville and marry him. He would continue to work and she could finish high school. I'm sure Brenda's parents weren't thrilled with the idea, but she did indeed return to Jacksonville as the new Mrs. Odom. It was 1967. She settled in to her new role easily. She kept a clean home, was a great cook, and had the gentle, loving spirit all men dream of.

1968 came like a lion. Vietnam was raging, and America was not sure how to handle it. Gene's friends were being drafted left and right. Gene just kept his head down and kept working. The Odom's hoped that the army wouldn't draft married men, but if needed, Gene would proudly serve his country.

Work got slow and Gene was laid off from his job. Gene looked around for more work, but the local economy was slow. The logical thing to do was fish. One day while Gene and Ronnie Van Zant were bank fishing, Ronnie offered him a job at the auto parts store he was managing for his brother in-law on 103rd street. His first day at work wasn't a great one, but it was memorable. While delivering parts in the company's VW Bug, the shifter got jammed in 2nd gear and cost $125 to repair. Ronnie threw his hands in the air and said, "Only you, Gene Odom." Gene decided not to tell Ronnie that he had been speed shifting when the problem started.

Ronnie had put together a band with four of his friends from the neighborhood including Gary Rossington, Allen Collins, and Bob Burns. During the summer of 1969 they were playing parties and small clubs. Due to the late night practices, Ronnie would ride the 10 miles to work with Gene and catch a little extra sleep. Gene would swing by Ronnie's apartment that Ronnie, his wife Nadine, and their little girl Tammy shared. One morning on their way to work, the left rear tire came off the rim of the delivery truck they were driving. The truck fish-tailed and was nearly on it's' side in the median on Emerson street. Ronnie woke up scared to death, but after seeing Gene gain control of the vehicle, he commented that Leroy Yarbarough would have been proud. Gene's legs were shaking, and his only comment was something about cleaning out his britches and getting a new tire.

Chapter 3
1961

"Rebel Flags and Racecars or just Gone with the Win"

THE CRICKETS WERE PLAYING THEIR song in a 1961 shantytown. Porch lights were on up and down the street. Laughter and country music could be heard somewhere in the distance. If you listened closely, you could hear the purr of a Chrysler engine that had been dropped into a 1934 Ford. Leroy Yarbrough was demonstrating his magic to two of his biggest fans. "Boys," he would say, "I'm gonna' drive this piece of crap like I stole it this Saturday night at the Jacksonville Speedway, and when they ask me how I done it in the winners circle, I'm gonna tell her that Gene Odom and Ronnie Van Zant taught me everything I know about racing junk cars on a dirt track. And when I reach over to kiss that beauty queen, I'm gonna tell her that Gene and Ronnie said hello." The little boys' eyes just lit up with excitement. To Gene and Ronnie, Leroy was the king. And at that very moment the king was doing something to the engine that was going to make every other driver at that track wish they had never heard the name Leroy Yarbrough.

Gene Odom was trying his best to stand as tall as he could when he spoke to his hero. "After you win this weekend, where will you race Leroy?" "I don't know for sure Gene, but I've been waiting my whole life for this day. This is all I've ever wanted to do and I'm gonna make the most of it. A man needs to follow his dreams."

Ronnie Van Zant had fallen silent. His young eyes looked off into a distance no one else could see. He was also a dreamer. He knew deep down in his heart that he too would live out his dreams. But for now it was pretty cool to be hanging around the garage with his best buddy and the man with a plan, the great Leroy Yarbrough.

The Sinclair Oil clock on the wall showed that it was nearly 10:00p.m. It was time for the boys to get home before somebody got worried. Annie Odum was a protective mother, and it was best if she didn't have to come looking for one of her kids.

Leroy made his dreams a reality in the coming years. He would win many races in his short career. In 1969, he won NASCAR's "Triple Crown" – the Daytona 500, the Firecracker 400, and the Southern 500 at Darlington. Nobody knows for sure what happened to Leroy. He had had too many wrecks to begin with, and it has been said that he was bitten by a tick on a camping trip in 1971. He developed Rocky Mountain spotted fever. He changed after that. The fire in his eyes was replaced by a sad distance. The surefooted cockiness was replaced by confusion.

Gene has told me of the day that he ran into Leroy in the summer of 1980. Leroy was picking up soda bottles in the very ditches that Gene himself had picked them out of twenty years earlier and bouncing around living with different family members. He recognized Gene and said, "I'm sure sorry to hear about our old buddy Ronnie. I'm just out here trying to get me some drinking money." Gene gave Leroy five dollars and left his childhood hero, carrying a desperate sadness. All the mental institutions and overeducated doctors in the country couldn't bring the great Leroy

Yarbrough back from the edge of darkness. He was truly one of the great ones. It seems odd to me that you don't hear his name mentioned in the NASCAR circles these days. Americans seem to only want to remember happy endings.

Gene gave me an old writing tablet that he had written poems in during his time of healing following the plane crash. I felt like the following poem fits well with this chapter.

Turn the Pages

I would like to go back to my boyhood days
Football and baseball and that old hot rod craze
A moonlit night on that cold dark lake
Scaring all the girls with that black rubber snake
If I could turn the pages back fifteen years
Before all the broken hearts and so many tears
Back to my bicycle and fishing pole
Skinny dipping in the old swimming hole
Before the tragedies that have occurred
Feelings that were shattered by just a few words
Back when I used to run home and check on my mother
Playing football and baseball with my older brothers
Those days are gone and they are over and done
Only in my mind will they ever return
If I could turn back the pages back fifteen years
Before all of the broken hearts
Before those many, many tears

written by Gene Odom (1977)

Chapter 4
1969

"Summer of Love?"

I N April 1969 Gene and Brenda's friends were still being drafted. (Ronnie Van Zant didn't need to worry because his ankle was full of pins necessary after a 1966 neighborhood football game injury.) Gene came home from the auto parts store on May 10, 1969 and was greeted with his draft papers. Brenda was scared and as Gene held his young wife, she looked up and asked "What are we going to do?" Gene just shrugged his shoulders and said, "Go whoop some Vietnamese butt". But before the butt- kicking could start, there was a certain hair stylist waiting with a pair of clippers at Fort Benning, Georgia. A lot of hair hit the floor that day and blue jeans were traded in for army fatigues. The next eight weeks would be tough. Georgia was breaking its own heat records during the summer of '69, and more than a few soldiers couldn't quite make the three mile run in formation. But just as always, the army turned a busload of softies into tough, trained killing machines. Following boot camp, Gene was allowed to go home to Brenda for six weeks. The time went by quickly. The first of August brought some good news. Instead of going to Vietnam, Gene would be sent to Germany for his final destination. Anywhere was better than a jungle with bullets flying around.

About 2:00 a.m. one morning, an army sergeant walked through the barracks calling out names. Gene's name was called and within the hour he was aboard a C-130 transport plane en route to Germany. The plane stopped at the coast of Spain, then Ireland, finally landing in Frankfurt, Germany. Because of his previous welding experience, he was given a job as a welder. That position had opened up for him because the pre-existing welder had lost his life due to a drug overdose. Following his stint as a welder he was given the opportunity to work as a parts runner. A parts runner was an individual that was responsible for making sure other mechanics had all of the parts required to do their individual jobs.

Gene had spent 1 year, 11 months, and ten days in Germany. During the last ten days of his stay, or his "clearing out time", as it was called, Gene was involved in an accident playing baseball. He had slid into third base and twisted his ankle to the point of being sent to Nuremburg Hospital. This resulted in a 10% disability income from the army.

Chapter 5
1972–1973

"Married with a Child"

U PON GETTING BACK TO AMERICA as a civilian, Gene got back into ironworking and Brenda worked as a waitress. In 1972, Brenda gave birth to their first daughter. She was like an angel sent down from heaven. Arriving two months premature, she fit in the palm of Gene's hand. She had beautiful red hair and was perfectly healthy. They named her Melissa Jean.

During this time, Gene worked all over Florida and Georgia as an ironworker. If he was at home, he would often work with his father on a small, wooden boat off the edge of Cumberland Island in the St. Johns River in the evening. This area of warm water fed into the ocean and was a significant running ground for shrimp. It was not uncommon to catch 700 to 800 lbs. a night using a simple cast net.

These years were happy ones. Even though the couple worked long, relentless hours, they were providing for their family. Please remember that in the early 1970s the economy was bad, there was a "so-called" energy crisis, and jobs weren't plentiful, especially in Northern Florida. Gene, like everyone else in his line of work had to travel to the work. Often, this meant going to places like northern Florida, Georgia, as well as Alabama.

It must have been an odd sensation to be headed to work and hear your childhood friends on the radio. Imagine leaving your place at 5:30 in the morning, heading to work and hearing the same boys you used to climb trees with, play baseball with, and fish with, as you travel through the early morning darkness. Lynyrd Skynyrd had arrived and music would never be the same. Gene Odom's life was about to be changed in a big way as well.

Chapter 6
1956

"Searchin' for Soda Bottles and Get Myself Some Dough"

THE LITTLE BOYS' FEET WERE pedaling slowly down Mull Street. He was focused on maintaining his balance as he delivered five more soda bottles to Claude's Midway grocery around the corner. It was early Saturday morning, the dew was still on the ground, and it was about to be a hot one.

The man in the white apron was Claude Hamner. He was the owner and was always glad to see the little boy. The wooden screen door screeched open, and Claude couldn't help but smile. Little Gene Odom was delivering his weekend recovery for pocket change. "I looked up and down all the ditches and parking lots as well as the dirt track. Maybe tomorrow morning I can find a few more." "Not bad work for a Saturday morning Gene. Here's your money, and the moon pie and the RC is on me. A working man like you needs to keep his strength up." The little boy just smiled as his small hands took the moon pie and ice cold drink. "Thank you. Maybe I can find a few more bottles tomorrow morning." Just as he turned for the door, a white Marita Bread delivery truck pulled up beside the little store. Gene got on his beat- up bicycle and pedaled for Ronnie Van Zant's house. Ronnie was already out near the street throwing a baseball up in the air.

"What's going on?" Ronnie asked. "Just gettin' rich three nickels at a time. What's up with you?" "Not much. Do you want to head over to the trees on the third turn of Speedway Park this afternoon? We can watch the race and maybe a tire will fly over the fence. We can sell it back to one of the drivers and make some folding money instead of a pocketful of nickels."

"Sounds like a plan, but if the plan falls apart we'll go fishin' when it cools off at the creek o.k.?"

Ronnie smiled. "I'll see you in a few hours. When dad get's home, I gotta help around the yard for a little while. I'll catch up with you as soon as I can get away".

Gene pedaled off. It would be a good day to just hang out and dream of being on that track with the great Lee Roy Yarborough and Wendell Scott...

Later, Ronnie and Gene found themselves fishing. No tires came over the fence that day, but the race had been exciting. The stands had been full even in the extreme Florida heat. Some guy named Bobby Allison had won the final race and had kissed the pretty girl with the crown and was given the trophy. That man was living the dream.

Watching the bobber in the nearly still water of Cedar River, Ronnie seemed to have something on his mind. "Gene, I'm not going to spend the rest of my life waiting for something to happen. I'm going to make something of myself one of these days." The Cedar River kept moving gently towards the St. John's River a few miles away. Some dreams fade away like current in a stream. Others burn like a light that won't burn out no matter what life throws at you. That's when a dream turns itself into a vision and a true vision won't die.

There has been speculation of just who Ronnie was referring to when he sang about the little boy picking up bottles early in the morning in "Curtis Loew". Most likely, the portion of the song that was sung as in first person experience was really about Gene. This song in particular had several characters in Ronnie's mind that he brought together to represent one little boy and one black guitarist. As a young boy, Gene has told me that Ronnie would have been too proud to be out in the community ditches picking up empty bottles to sell. Ronnie's parents had good jobs so he probably didn't need to worry about extra spending money. Gene on the other hand, had come from an entire litter of brothers and sisters. He had to do some extra work even at that age if he was going to have any change in his empty pockets. The Van Zant's back porch was often one of the places Gene would find some empty bottles to redeem for a little spending money.

Ed King, Skynyrd guitarist has said that the unusual spelling of "Loew" was his idea. When he was writing the liner notes for the Second Helping album, he decided to name the character after Loew's Theater-thus giving the old bluesman a Jewish name.

Tom Ferrell, one of Gene and Ronnie's boyhood friends, has been helpful in bringing the old neighborhood to life. The west side neighborhood, or shantytown as it was sometimes called, was a mix of working people. But, just because people worked hard, didn't necessarily mean that all of life's basics were covered. Several of the homes in that immediate area had dirt floors, and many of the homes didn't have indoor plumbing. Gene's grandmother, for instance, lived just around the corner from his parent's house, and she didn't have indoor plumbing. Because of the size of Gene's family, private space was hard to come by. Fortunately, The Odoms had an older bachelor neighbor named Gordon Hess. That gentleman liked Gene and saw the potential in the young boy. He fed Gene his supper nearly every evening and allowed Gene to take his baths there as well as wash his clothes. Like I mentioned earlier, the people in the neighborhood looked after each other.

Chapter 7
1974-1976

"You Can't Always Get What You Want"

B Y THE SUMMER OF 1974, Skynyrd was selling out arenas all over the United States. During an off week, Ronnie stopped by to see how his old friend was doing. When he found out that Gene was out of work at the moment, he insisted that Gene go out on the road as a bodyguard and security officer to make extra money. Gene accepted the offer. Brenda was pregnant again with their youngest daughter Christie, and they could certainly use the money. For some of 1974 and the first part of 1975, Gene worked with Skynyrd when the construction market was dry.

Ronnie called Gene at home in the late spring of 1975 with yet another job opportunity. Peter Rudge was Skynyrd's manager, but he was the Rolling Stones' tour manager. The Stones had a need for a more personal security guard and Ronnie told Rudge about Gene's work with Skynyrd and his consistent dependability. Gene boarded a plane headed for New York City. Ronnie had told him to bring his pistol. When he arrived in New York with a .357 magnum in his suitcase, he didn't know what to expect. His new job would be to serve the Rolling Stones on the "Tour of the Americas." His primary job was to quietly glide around the people in the Stones' inner circle and ensure safety and privacy. The new gig paid well, but this was not the type of people Gene Odom was comfortable spending time with. Mick Jagger and company weren't the type of men you could talk to about fishing or NASCAR. It was doubtful these people had ever even wet a worm on a hook. Instead, they seemed to live a lifestyle of excess and exile from the very type of people that Gene Odom was from. During one of his stays in New York, Gene was witness to that city's first gay liberation parade. That day over 300,000 men and women shouted, "Two, Four, Six, Eight; we don't overpopulate!" Gene Odom must have been wondering what in the world a confederate soldier like himself was doing breathing the same air as 300,000 flaming homosexuals.

As soon as the Rolling Stones were in Jacksonville to play a show, Gene decided to stay home and not continue on the road with them. With two young baby girls and a wife at home, this decision made sense at the time. It was good to be home with those that he loved the most. Gene got off the plane at the Jacksonville airport and never returned. Working for the Rolling Stones had been an eye opening opportunity, but he didn't fit in with these people and felt lonely and isolated from the people he loved and cared about.

One of the problems with spending time on the road as a traveling iron worker and then working on the road with two of the largest acts in popular music was that Gene had developed the need to pull away from everyone, including those closest to him. He started fishing nearly every evening, playing too much pool at the pool hall, and had also developed a gambling habit. It wasn't long until Gene was given his walking papers from Brenda.

Chapter 8
1976

"Walking Through Richmond"

THE TARTER FAMILY DIDN'T HAVE the extras that most Americans take for granted. They were a third generation mining family nestled deep in the mountains of Virginia surrounded by trees, beautiful valleys, and expansive blue sky. The neighbors were either family members or friends that felt like family. The men worked thousands of feet below in the coal mine as the women maintained the home and greeted each moment with a silent prayer of faith to keep their husbands safe.

Young David Tarter was a simple young man that loved his parents, loved his friends, and loved the Lynyrd Skynyrd band. He had done some research in the school library for his creative writing class on the band, their sound, and the lyrics. He had inadvertently discovered a fan mail address for the band and began writing to someone with a Jacksonville address that he would soon realize was actually Mrs. Marion Virginia Hicks Van Zant. Mrs. Van Zant could relate to the boy. After all, she had three of her own. He was a dreamer. She encouraged dreams. He loved his family but felt trapped and isolated in the mountains. She had felt the same way until Lacy Van Zant rescued her and gave her a chance to see the world outside of her own small town. David Tarter had heard on his small box radio that the band would be coming to his state later in the spring. Even though he couldn't afford to go and didn't have the transportation if he could, he told Mrs. Van Zant how excited he was, knowing that his heroes would at least be visiting his state. To David, this was truly an honor, and he felt pride and excitement knowing his favorite band would give Richmond a magical night of music, southern pride, and rebel flags.

Marion put the boy's letter in her apron pocket and went to work making dinner for her family. Today would be a special day for her. Ronnie, Donnie, Johnnie, Marlene, and Darlene would all be sitting in their appointed seats at the dinner table with her and her husband Lacy. Even though life had gotten much faster lately, with two boys already cutting quite a swath in the music business and young Johnnie showing the beginning signs of being just like his brothers, she just wanted her family together as often as possible. Her daughter Marlene had met a young man named Bill Hodge. She was crazy in love with the young man and planned on getting married in the spring of the following year. Darlene was also about to step out into the world as a young adult. It wouldn't be long until the Van Zant home would be a lot emptier with only the parents left to take care of each other. Mr. and Mrs. Van Zant were happy and very proud of each of their children. They were excited for their kids to discover the world and all it held for each of them. But at the same time, they were both sad to know that soon all would be quiet on the home front.

Dinner was over and the family went out on the porch to relax. Ronnie stayed behind in the kitchen to help his mother clean off the table and finish what was left of the apple cobbler. She reached into her apron and pulled out the letter from David Tarter and put it in

Ronnie's hand. Ronnie read the letter as his mom put the pressure cooker back in the cabinet.

"Ronnie, I would really appreciate it if you would do something special for that young boy in Virginia. You, Gary, and Allen are his heroes. Remember how you used to follow Lee Roy Yarborough around like a puppy?" Ronnie stared at the letter on the kitchen table as his mom told him how important it was to reach out to his fans when he could.

Ronnie put the letter in his pants pocket and followed his mom out to the porch to be with his dad, brothers, and little sisters. Later that afternoon he would be telling his own wife and daughter goodbye as he hit the road again.

Richmond was ready for the party as March rolled around the corner with the promise of a warming spring attached to it. David Tarter was finishing up the day's chores and planning on listening to the radio hoping for some possible live interviews with Skynyrd band members before the evening show. David's mother opened the back screen door and told him to come to the house and get cleaned up because they would be having company for supper. David assumed it was someone from the church coming over to plan a spring event, possibly an Easter egg hunt.

The black limousines snaked through the Virginia countryside quietly as the locals looked up in total surprise, wondering where the procession was headed and why. Ronnie, Gary Rossington, Allen Collins, and Gene were in the front car. Gary looked out the darkened window at the streams, hills, and dogwood tree's wondering quietly if he and his friends were the ones that were missing out on what life has to offer. Artimus Pyle, Billy Powell, Leon Wilkeson and Steve Gaines were in the second car following their leaders to make a teenager's dream come true.

As the car cruised up the long gravel driveway, Ronnie cautioned his friends to make sure that David's parents were told by all that their son would be well taken care of.

David could hear the family dog outside barking more than normal. He could hear the concern in his dog's voice. As he went to the front door and walked out on the front porch, he saw the big city cars in his driveway. The doors opened and Ronnie Van Zant began walking towards his house with Gary on the left and Allen on the right side of him. Gene Odom was up against the car watching as Ronnie happily carried out his mother's wishes for her pen pal.

David's heart nearly leaped out of his throat when Ronnie smiled and said, "Hi David, we heard that your mom makes some of the best fried chicken around here, so we thought we would stop by and check it out. Would you like to go to our show with us later on tonight?" The rowdy south was about to walk through Richmond, Virginia, one more time with the amps turned up, rebel flags and all. The band didn't need spotlights that evening because David Tarter's smile would light up the entire auditorium. Every young man needs to listen to his mother.

Chapter 9
1977

"Life is so Strange with its Changes Yes Indeed"

THERE IS NOT MUCH ON this earth more painful than a failed marriage. As hurtful as it was, Gene found solace in knowing that he would always be part of his sweet daughters' lives. Brenda, being the loving woman that she is, allowed Gene to be as much a part of their daughters' lives as his schedule would allow. It is also important to know that Gene put the gambling and the pool halls behind him. As far as the fishing goes, Mr. Odom has declined to comment.

Ronnie had a nice bass boat. He and Gene were out on the lake talking one afternoon. The fishing wasn't great that day and it allowed the two friends to get caught up on what was going on in their lives. Ronnie was honest with Gene. He told him that the drugs and alcohol were out of control and things needed to change across the board with the band. Because of their lifestyles, the live shows were becoming sloppy. The band was also going to need a solid album if they planned on being around much longer as an arena act. Skynyrd's last few albums had not proven to be radio friendly. He asked Gene to go on the road with him and help his friends get the problem under some type of control. He put one thousand dollars in Gene's tee shirt pocket and told him to catch all of his bills up. Skynyrd was getting ready to record a live album in Atlanta and it was crucial that the "cleaning up" process begin immediately.

In today's world, rock stars and Hollywood types check into a high- end facility that offers counseling, exercise, private chefs, and privacy in dealing with such problems. We are talking about the Lynyrd Skynyrd band, and that's not how things were done in 1977. Gene started weaning the band off slowly. He would go to the backstage area and pour half of the whiskey, beer, champagne, and wine out before and during the show. Slowly but surely, the band started to play tighter. Fewer fights among band members were occurring, and minds became much clearer. The band had lived a lifestyle dedicated to excessive partying and violence, and finally, for a brief moment anyway, things looked promising. Proof of this is on the "One More from the Road" album recorded at the Fox Theater in Atlanta. This record includes Steve Gaines in the new lineup. He had taken over as the third guitar player replacing Ed King. (Mr. King had abruptly walked away from his duties as guitarist. Life on the road with Skynyrd had proven to be more than he had signed on for.) You can feel the freshness in the music. Skynyrd had turned a corner towards a better way and Gene Odom was looking down the barrel of a new and exciting career.

Gene had been living with Leon Wilkeson, the bass player in Skynyrd, until he could find a place of his own. It was awkward being a bachelor after being married for so long, but he slowly adapted. A new residence, a new career, and a new vision helped balance the overpowering changes in Gene's life. Even with all of the excitement, when a man loses the warmth of his family, he can be completely alone in a room full of ten thousand people. That is one bullet that is unavoidable.

Chapter 10
1977

"We Still Remember You"

THE SUMMER OF 1977 WAS spent on the road touring and alternately working on the upcoming "Street Survivors" album. While the band was in final days of production in Atlanta, Gene went to Ronnie's lakefront residence just south of Jacksonville on Brickyard road to work on a small wooden bridge in the driveway. The structure itself was framed with some old telephone poles. Through the years, rain and settling had pushed the bridge into the ground and it needed some dirt around it for support as well as aesthetics. Ronnie came home for a few weeks to rest before the tour began.

The band did several weeks of shows promoting the new album. The evening the band flew towards Greenville, South Carolina from Lakeland, Florida, Gene and some other crew and band members were playing poker near the right window of the plane. Gene looked out the window as a ball of fire shot from the engine. He went to the cockpit and told the pilot to, "Turn the plane around. Something happened to the right engine." The pilot said there was nothing wrong and to be seated. (Gene has said that the plane was "missing" every now and then.) From that point on, the rest of the flight was uneventful. The plane landed safely in Greenville. The pilot informed Gene that the problem was in the magneto on the right engine and that things would be taken care of.

The following morning, Gene got up early to speak to the pilot. He was told at the front desk of the hotel that they had left for the airport. Gene arrived to find the pilot and the co-pilot working on the plane. Gene felt more than a little frustration knowing that the plane did need to be repaired and a band- aid was not what was needed. After all, as Gene has said, when an airplane is 10,000 feet in the air there is no room for mistakes or malfunctions.

October 20th arrived in Greenville. It had been a relaxing day for the members of the Skynyrd entourage. Around 2:00 p.m. that afternoon, arrangements had been made to have everyone enroute to the plane. Several band members, including Cassie Gaines, and crew members had voiced their concern about the safety of the chartered plane and they were willing to purchase a commercial flight to Baton Rouge. The pilots had convinced the road manager that all issues had indeed been resolved and there was no need for concern.

The Convair 240 left at approximately 4:55 that afternoon. The leaves had started changing, the early evening sky was a brilliant blue, but there was a terrible storm ahead. While in flight, Ronnie was taking a nap on the floor beneath Gary and Allan's feet. He had been up partying through the night and was exhausted. A poker game was deep in play, some of the girls were reading magazines, and Steve Gaines and Dean Kilpatrick were discussing album art at a table near the front of the plane. At 6:30 p.m. at 12,000 feet, the engines on both sides of the plane began to sputter. As the engines were running out of fuel, the plane would "fishtail". Gene went to the front to speak to the pilots and was told to make sure everyone was strapped in. They were looking for an open area to make a "belly landing," but there were no areas open enough to land a plane on. At that moment, Gene, having a background in ironworking and military, knew that a 68,000 pound plane fully loaded and out of gas was not about to have a gentle belly landing.

The plane made her final descent, and Gene did as he was told. As he headed back toward the cockpit to cuss the pilots out one more time and tell them he hoped they lived through this so he could personally beat them both to death, he realized that they weren't going to make it to a field. The plane had changed its descent angle to a much sharper 52 degree downward direction, and the ground was coming up fast. He picked Ronnie up off the floor and threw him between Gary and Allen and gave him a pillow. "Ronnie, we're about to crash. Help me get this seat belt on you." Ronnie, being groggy from his sleep, thought Gene was joking. He said "Come on man, I need to get some rest. Don't be joking around with me." Gene slapped him in the face and said, "I ain't joking! Put your head between your legs!" At that instant, someone yelled, "Trees!" Gene turned to try and run for his seat, but at that instant, impact began and he was thrown through the fuselage under the right wing and engine: the very engine that had caused the disaster.

Rescue wouldn't show up for 45 minutes because air traffic control was not given proper coordinates. The plane had been lost to radar and the pilots had made no attempt to give direction prior to the crash. The forest surrounding the crash was dense with Mississippi pines growing right in the middle of a muddy swamp.

A local farmer's daughter had just gotten home from work. Miss Jaqueline Cooper had already heard on the local radio that a chartered plane carrying the Lynyrd Skynyrd Band had crashed somewhere in the area.

Miss Cooper's father told her that he had just heard a metallic crunching noise off in the distance. He and his daughter walked across their fields in that direction. As they walked up on the crash site, they saw the carnage was immense. The young lady ran back home for help and the father ran back to the barn to get some tools. On the way back, the pair ran into a Mr. Johnnie Mote, a local farmer, and his helper. They were on their way to find the crash site because band member Artimus Pyle and two crew members, Marc Frank and Kenneth Paden, Jr. had stopped by Mr. Mote's house asking for help. They had been soaked in what appeared to be blood and were in bad shape.

At this point, rescue workers and police were on their way as well as other local residents. One family in particular who lived on the adjoining property was already at the site giving aid to the survivors. This must have been a terrifying and heart wrenching scene to happen upon. However this young lady and her brother assessed the situation and began helping the injured. Shortly after, Mr. Mote returned with makeshift equipment to help the injured. Trapped within the twisted fuselage in the area behind the cockpit, there was a pile of bodies including Ronnie Van Zant, Steve Gaines, Cassie Gaines, Allan Collins, Garry Rossington, Dean Kilpatrick, and Kevin Ellison. Mr. Mote ripped the fuselage open with an axe and started removing the injured. When they realized that Ronnie, Dean, and Cassie couldn't be helped, they were laid off to the side of the wreckage under a tree. Steve Gaines apparently had not passed away at this time. He mentioned that he was cold. He was wrapped in Miss Cooper's coat to help him stay warm. Steve was badly bruised across his chest, probably from the table that he had been sitting behind at the time of the crash. This more than likely caused serious internal bleeding that would give him the sensation of being cold and ultimately take his life. Four ambulances had gotten stuck in the mud trying to get to the wreckage. Mr. Mote began pulling four-wheel wheel drive pickup trucks to the plane with his tractor. The injured were loaded in the back of the trucks and the trucks were pulled back to the road by the tractor. The trucks were unloaded, and the broken bodies were moved into the ambulances and taken down a narrow country road to be transported to the hospital. The hospital was overwhelmed. Several survivors were transported to a Jackson Mississippi Hospital one hundred and three miles away by a National Guard helicopter including Gary Rossington, Allan Collins and Gene Odom.

Bill Hodge is married to Ronnie's little sister Marlene. She was seven months pregnant with their daughter Virginia Anne in October of 1977. The news of the crash was trickling into Jacksonville via the radio, television, and telephone. Upon hearing of the tragedy, Marlene was devastated. Johnny Van Zant picked her up outside of the apartment that she and Bill shared and took her to their parents' house. Hours passed before the family finally found out who survived the crash. Bill took Marlene to the hospital late that evening to be calmed down and checked out by a doctor to ensure that their baby was all right. When Ronnie died, part of Mr. and Mrs. Van Zant died with him. Mrs. Van Zant never worked or drove her car again. Although she loved all of her children equally, she would never be the same. Her heart was broken. Weeks would pass by before Gene Odom would find out that his beloved fishing buddy was gone. The dream was over.

"Cold Dark Mississippi Night"

It was at 12,000 feet when we fell from the sky
As of this day I still don't know why
Sometimes I question my Maker's decision
But what I see in this life could just be an illusion

On a cold dark Mississippi night
Angels came holding a glowing light
They took some and left others behind
To live in this life till' their chosen time

I owe not much to the people I'm around
But I sure owe a lot to this Mississippi town
Her people came through water and mud
To lend a helping hand wherever they could

Looking at this place from the air I've heard
You can see the shadow of a great big bird
That flew these parts not too long ago
With music and song that would make me glow
On a cold dark Mississippi night
Angels came holding a light
They took some and left others behind
To live in this world till' their chosen time

Gene Odom

Chapter 11
1977

"I Was Still There, Just Like Before When the Free Bird Hit the Ground"

HAVING BEEN TRANSPORTED FROM MISSISSIPPI to Jacksonville Hospital, Gene would need several months to heal before he could begin piecing his life back together. His left eye had been burned as well as his arm and hand. The C5 disk in his upper spine had been broken, his ribs were broken and fractured, and he had massive head injuries resulting in brain damage. During his stay, he lost over forty pounds and became terribly weak. To help the pain, he had been receiving Demerol as a pain reliever, but this medication made him hallucinate. The skin grafts helped hide the scars on his body, but his heart was about to be broken. After finally leaving the hospital, he was taken to the graveyard in Orange Park to visit Ronnie. During all of this time, he had not been told of Ronnie's death. At that moment, the post- traumatic stress, the anguish, and all of the internal pain just came upon him like a train. He sat there in front of that cold stone for a long time trying to get a handle on those feelings, only to realize that the good Lord and time itself were the only answers to what appeared to be an insurmountable problem.

Because he had been acting as the bands security guard, Gene felt guilty. He asked himself all of the "what if" questions. What if he had stopped the band from getting on the plane in the first place? What if he had demanded in no uncertain terms that the plane be repaired before being used again? What if he hadn't put Ronnie in the seat between Gary and Allen? The world would keep on turning, but these questions didn't have answers then, and thirty plus years later, they still don't. Sometimes we just have to accept reality and move on with our lives. There are times, as unfortunate as it may seem, that God does His work in very mysterious, often very painful ways. The important thing is that He is there for us, and this is the very source from where we find the strength to carry on. Upon writing Gene's story, I begin to realize that everyone on that plane including the pilot weren't what you could call seasoned adults. Instead, it was a plane full of young, very talented kids that probably felt bulletproof. I can't help but wonder what in the world the management for Lynyrd Skynyrd was doing during all of this. Who would knowingly allow a plane full of innocent people to be traveling around the country on a worn out plane?

I know that by now you feel like all of the poetry I am including in this little book should probably have been sent to Hallmark Cards and Gifts. But, I wanted you, the reader, to see some of what I have been allowed to see as well. Allen Collins wrote the following poem in Gene's spiral notebook.

Untitled

They said eight hours would decide if my arm
    would live or die
I was laying there with my arm in the air
Wondering if I was going to lose it
My arm was blue and cold as the winter sky
When I looked at it I began to cry
Doctors and nurses not giving a damn
When in through the door burst a man named Sam
With blood in his eyes and a scalpel in hand
He rushed me to the OR room and began
To save the part of me that makes me be me
With thanks from above and a doctor friend
Now it's all over
I'm going to play again

written by Allen Collins (1977)

Chapter 12
1977

"Questions without answers"

G ENE DIDN'T KNOW HOW TO feel. How does one walk away from such pain? Do you feel blessed that you survived and that you were spared? Or do you feel cursed because you lived? I can't imagine the process that every one of these people had to go through.

If you are reading this, you remember where you were when it happened. I have always been one to resist other people's ramblings about what Skynyrd would have done if things could have stayed on course. I instead, would rather look at what they accomplished. Every time I'm driving down the road and hear today's flavor of the week, I hear Ed King, Allen Collins, and Garry Rossington deep in the mix. Nashville only wishes they could have something close to what Skynyrd was. You and me, we have the music or the music has us. I don't know which. But one thing is for sure, they were not some lightweight band that needed other people's songs or Nashville writers. Before I go any further with this book, I just wanted to confirm to you the reader that I love and appreciate every note they played. Their music changed my life, and there is a pretty good chance that if you're reading this now, you have driven that country road listening to some "Tuesday's Gone" or "Gimme' Back my Bullets" as the sun was going down, thinking at that moment there just isn't any music in the whole universe close to this or as good as this. And as far as I'm concerned, you are absolutely right… But this book is about my very dear friend Gene Odom.

In my house, I have a poem on the wall written by Gene that speaks to me on a daily basis. Maybe all of us take the day for granted, including what it is measured by. Before you go any farther with this story, read this poem and then read it again.

Time

There is a thing, a mist is all
Better known as time
It only travels in one way
Never to unwind
We look at our watch to tell
What time it is now
Only to wonder, "Where has time went?"
So fast, so silent, slow down
Yesterday I was eighteen
Today I'm twenty- nine
Tomorrow I'll be thirty- five
Next year I'll be old man time
We're living our lives way too fast
And one day we'll regret
The way we let time slip away
And the times we can't forget.
Friends, our time here is limited
An angel holds the key
So let's slow down our living
It's best for you and me

Gene Odom

Billy, Allen & Ronnie

Allen, Gary & Ronnie

Allen & Ronnie

Allen, Ronnie & Artimus

Allen, Ronnie & Artimus Pyle

Allen, Ronnie & Gary Rossington

Ronnie Van Zant

Ronnie Van Zant

Ed King & Gary Rossington

Ed King & Leon Wilkeson

Allen Collins

Allen Collins

Gary Rossington

High School where Gary and Ronnie attended

Charlie Daniels & Gene Odom

Gene Odom

Dave Hlubek, Ron Isabell & Gene Odom

Ronnie Van Zant, Bob Burnes, Gary Rossington, Allen Collins and
Larry Junstrom

Gary Rossington and Gene Odom somewhere
on the road in the 80's

Two of Scott Coner's closest friends, Gene Odom and lifelong
friend, Johnny Burbrink 2009

Chapter 13
1980

"Don't Misunderstand Me"

THE DOCTORS FELT LIKE GENE should have died. After all, he had been in a plane crash. He had chemical burns up his arm, his right eye had been burned, and he had a massive hole in his head. The C5 disk in his neck, and the L4 and L5 in his back were broken. Additionally, he had compression fractures in all of his vertebrate, and his ribs had been fractured. Skin graphs were done to improve the scars on the side of his face and arms, but it was going to take a long time for his internal scars to heal.

The following three years would be a season of healing and rehabilitation. Upon leaving the hospital, he stayed with a girlfriend and her father because he couldn't move around on his own. After a few weeks, he moved into a buddy's house near the naval base until he could get strong enough to get back into iron working.

Gene's burns were the first of their kind in Florida to be treated with the Jobst Pressure Garment. This "garment" was actually a type of bandage that kept constant pressure on his skin while still allowing it to breathe. It covered not only his arms and midsection, but also his head, which was wrapped up like Boris Karloff in the

"Mummy". During this time he had gained enough strength to go to the bank. On the way back to his car, Gene was greeted by some of Jacksonville's finest who had been tipped off that there was a robbery taking place. Guns were put away, but a newspaper story was run the next day stating, "This Man is not a Bank Robber!" It would be a few more months until he would only be required to wear the bandages at night.

The 1980's arrived with a hollow cry. We lost John Lennon very suddenly just as he stepped back into the spotlight from spending time away with his family. The whole world was changing, and music was changing right along with it. Guitar anthems and songs with lyrics that touched our hearts were replaced by soulless, meaningless pop confections, driven by robotic techno beats. People we related to because they reminded us of ourselves were replaced by a face- changing moon- walker with a fondness for children.

Meanwhile, Gary and Allen were realizing that they couldn't sit around the house for the rest of their lives waiting on royalty checks to hit the mailbox. They started a band fronted by a female singer from Indiana named Dale Krantz and got back into what they did best. The Rossington Collins Band was Gary, Allen, Billy, and Leon, with Barry Harwood on guitar and Derreck Hess on drums. The first album was an immediate hit. The single, "Don't Misunderstand Me" was getting heavy rotation and ticket sales were excellent. The phoenix had risen from its fiery ashes.

Gary Rossington asked Gene to be the road manager for the band. This allowed him the opportunity to be with his friends and continue the internal healing process. While in the hospital, he had started a small collection of poetry and short stories. At the time, he had no intention of releasing a book; it was just a form of "self-induced therapy." However, as time passed he continued to write about his time spent with Lynyrd Skynyrd and his friendship with

Ronnie. While at a Virginia Beach show with Rossington Collins, he spoke to a group of young girls about his little "book." One girl in particular, Brenna Barry, felt like Gene needed to follow through with completing and releasing the book for others to read. The book, "Lynyrd Skynyrd I'll Never Forget You," was about to become a reality.

Also during this time, Gene would meet the next Mrs. Gene Odom. Lori Timmel and Gene seemed to click right off the bat. And after three long and painful years, it appeared that things were starting to proceed in a direction that was finally both fulfilling and happy.

The tour promoting the new Rossington Collins album had been a success and the album itself would eventually go gold. Gary and Dale Krantz had fallen in love and would soon be married. However, during the recording process of the follow- up album things started to fall apart internally for the band. Allen went back home because the drugs had become too prevalent and the sound just wasn't there anymore. He had also lost his wife and unborn child due to complications during her pregnancy. The sophomore attempt of the Rossington Collins band was greeted with very little enthusiasm and lackluster sales. Gene Odom had also walked away from the band during that time in the studio refusing to be a part of a group of people that had lost all focus primarily due to drug use. For the road manager, these people, his childhood friends, had become unmanageable.

Something else happened during this season of Gene's life that was and still is very painful. Richard, Gene's older brother, died mysteriously while in the Duval County jail. The version that was released from the police station to the Odom family was suicide. Gene doesn't believe it happened that way at all. Richard Odom had been in and out of jail so many times it is hard to conceive, but he wasn't unhappy, and he certainly wasn't going to be taking his own life in a jail cell. He was just mean. He not only refused to walk away from a fight, but would often actually go looking for one. If he didn't like the way you looked at him, he would attack. If he saw an interracial couple, he would attack. Richard didn't care how big a man was, or if he had a gun or any other type of weapon. Richard would simply attack.

Gene was told by the authorities that Richard had hanged himself by an in-mate's sweater. They went on to say that Richard had been addicted to cocaine and alcohol, therefore causing his depression. Richard was not depressed at this point in his life. He obviously was still having problems with the Jacksonville police, but his wife had recently given birth to a son, and Richard was very happy and proud. He was looking forward to the future with his wife and little boy. There is no doubt in any of the Odoms' minds that Richard was choked to death by the guards in the jail. There is also no doubt that there was a cover- up concerning Richard's abrupt death. One key point for the record: If you hang yourself, your neck will either break or be severely damaged. Richard's neck, according to Gene, was not damaged in any significant way that would have caused death.

By the time Gene's family was given permission to view Richard's body, rigor mortis had already set in. Gene feels very strongly that those people involved needed time to establish a lie. The end result was terrible for the family. The Odom family felt it was obviously a cover-up, but years have passed and nothing can be done about it now. This was just one more item on the long list of hurtful things Gene would need to find a way to recover from.

It is also interesting to point out that in the late 1960s, another one of Gene's older brothers, "Red," was serving time for bank robbery. Gene has told me that Ronnie modeled the song "The Four Walls of Raiford" after "Red" Odom. The Odom family had experienced more than a fair share of heartache and disappointment.

Chapter 14
1984

"Phases and Stages"

ALLAN COLLINS AND GENE HAD remained close friends since childhood, and it wasn't surprising to anyone when Allan asked Gene to be the road manager for the newly formed Allan Collins Band. The band started on a smaller scale than Rossington Collins or Skynyrd, but people seemed to not only enjoy but appreciate the music. They began promoting the first album in small clubs around the South and the Midwest.

Allan had provided Gene with several photos to include in his book, but more importantly, he instructed Gene to have a written document signed by all band members and notarized allowing Gene to use the name Lynyrd Skynyrd in the book and on the title. Ten thousand books were printed and sales were going well. Gene also had 2,500 Allan Collins Band T-shirts made to sell on the road. Unfortunately, Allen fired the lead singer in the band, Jimmy Dougherty, because of severe alcohol problems and Gene was stuck with a truckload of books and obsolete shirts overnight without warning. Obviously, Genes' first reaction would be to kick Allan's butt, but Allan was certain that he would be back on the road promoting both the new album and Gene's merchandise within weeks. He promised Gene that his investment was as safe as it could be and not to worry. Problem was, the irony of Allen Collins firing his lead singer when his own abusive addictions were getting the best of him. Allen had never truly slowed down his excessive behavior. He was still binge drinking and doing cocaine on a regular basis.

During the time Allen needed to locate a new singer, tragedy touched his life again. He was involved in an auto accident, leaving him paralyzed from the chest down. A female passenger lost her life. They had apparently been driving to the liquor store to buy beer. Complications from this accident put Allen in a convalescent home for the remainder of his life before he eventually passed away.

Once again, Gene returned to life as an iron worker. His wife Lori had a good job working in downtown Jacksonville at Blue Cross Blue Shield. Life went back to some type of normalcy for the couple and Gene was given the opportunity to be a husband with a normal job again. Times were good. There is something to be said about working all week and coming home to the woman you love. The little things, like dinner at home, watering flowers in the evening, and mowing the lawn don't mean as much to us if we haven't lived a life on the road the way that Gene had.

The next year was spent getting caught up on bills and doing work around the house. For the first time in years, Gene was experiencing what too many of us take for granted: just living. And you know what? Just living is a pretty sweet way to spend your time.

Gene's oldest daughter Mellissa was a teenager and she was having some trouble at her mother's home adapting to her mom's new husband. She asked if she could move in with Gene and Lori. The couple was more than happy to make room for the little girl. After certain accommodations were made, Mellissa and her pet cockatiel had a new home. This must have truly been a blessing for Gene. He was now being given the opportunity to be a full time dad, have a forty hour a week job, and spend time with a wife that he just adored.

Chapter 15
1985

"Good and bad times"

A s 1985 WAS GETTING STARTED, Gene had been having severe pain episodes with his left eye. He had several cornea grafts over the years because of the damage done in the plane wreck, but nothing seemed to help long term. Gene was sent to a specialist at the University of Florida and it was decided to insert steroids directly into the cornea using a needle. Gene has told me that he has never endured pain like that before in his life. He said he could hear the popping sound of the steroid as it went into his eye. This procedure would leave him in the corner of the room on his knees blinded by pain.

A few months later, Gene was having terrible pain in his eye again. He had developed glaucoma and due to previous damage his ducts were not allowing any pressure to be released. He went back to the specialist who decided to make an incision on the eye to alleviate the pressure. Again, this would only be a short term application. The pressure returned because the incision closed. During the night, Gene became delirious with the pressure and the pain it caused. That evening, Gene was taken to the emergency room, and the eye had to be removed.

1987 was a milestone year for all who had been directly involved with the Lynyrd Skynyrd band. Charlie Daniels would be having his Volunteer Jam in Nashville, Tennessee, that year. Gary Rossington had talked with Billy Powell and Judy Van Zant and it was agreed that a ten show tribute tour would be arranged, starting at the Nashville Jam. As the surviving members walked out on the stage, Nashville, Tennessee lost its mind. Johnnie Van Zant, Ronnie's little brother, had been chosen to take on the lead vocals for the band. The raw emotion in that room was palpable. It has been said that you could feel the very presence of Mr. Ronnie Van Zant that evening, and that presence was one filled with love and pride. Gene was also with the band for these ten shows selling T-shirts and the "Lynyrd Skynyrd I'll Never Forget You" books. Following these shows, Gene went back home to his wife and Melissa. He turned forty years old that winter. Lori had a surprise birthday party for him. It sounds like a typical birthday for most of us, but Lori told me that it was the first time she saw Gene cry. He had never had a birthday cake or a birthday party until that day.

As the '80s were shooting by, Lori had been mentioning her desire to have children to Gene often. These comments were always met with a very stern answer from Gene. It wasn't going to happen, and there was no reason to discuss it. Little did Gene Odom know that maybe a little bit of understanding and communication, possibly the gift of a small lap dog, may have gone a very long way.

Chapter 16
1985

"Dream's I'll Never See"

GENE CAME HOME AFTER A hard, hot day of work in the Florida sun. He was tired and looking forward to a shower and a look at the days' newspaper, followed by a quiet supper with his wife and Mellissa. Maybe later he could sit out on the porch with a nice glass of sweet tea and relax as the sun drifted away leaving nothing but a cool Atlantic breeze and some peace of mind. Lately, he had been getting some strange chills even when he was in the sun working. He told himself it was just his body fighting the intense heat, and he hoped he was right. He was looking forward to spending the following week with his friend Danny Joe Brown and the Molly Hatchet Band. Danny Joe had called Gene about a month earlier inviting him to go out on a short tour with the band and sell his books at the shows. Danny had heard about the Allen Collins incident and was aware of the financial shape it had left Gene in. It would be good to move some books. It would also be good to get back on the road for a few days. Gene Odom definitely had those traveling bones.

As the week finally came to a close, Gene was packed and ready to see a few new towns and hear some "Bounty Hunter" at a very loud decibel. Life was good. Following the first concert though, Gene was feeling more than just a little sluggish. Sweat was pouring off of his arms like he had just stepped out of a swimming pool. Rather than have a late night dinner with the band, Gene returned to his hotel room. Something was wrong. A few more hours passed and Gene was going from one extreme to the other. For a while he was burning hot, only to be freezing cold a few minutes later. He was aware that he needed to see his doctor. Thankfully he was in Atlanta and, with any luck, he could be home in three or four hours. The trip home was a nightmare, but as he rolled into his driveway, his wife was waiting anxiously prepared to get him to the hospital. Blood was taken, blood pressure was checked, Gene was examined from head to toe. No one could assess the situation. The one thing that the doctors did agree on was that the spikes in his temperature were going to kill him. After three days of this, he was told by his doctor that he needed to make certain that things were in order, because at this rate he wasn't going to be amongst the living but a few more days. Gene could only lie in that lonely hospital bed and wonder. He had been asked over and over if he had tried any new food, new medicine, new anything! All of a sudden, he realized that the only significant change in his life was his little girl moving in with him with her pet bird. As soon as this bit of news was laid upon the table, the doctors knew what the problem was. Gene had contracted Parrot fever from Melissa's cockatiel. The right medicine was administered, and Mr. Odom was going to live to see another day. It is amazing what a striking difference a few hours can make. Just a short while before, Gene was trying to get his head around dying, and now he was about to get his street clothes back on and walk out the doors of the hospital. As the fog lifted from his mind, he made a mental note not to take the little things in life for granted, like breathing, walking, and looking forward to the next sunrise. Besides, Melissa was moving out and moving back in with her mother and sister. She might need her dad again soon.

Chapter 17
May 19, 1989

"I don't know if it's Tuesday or August"

LORI HAD SEEMED DISTANT LATELY. Gene could only assume that she was having some "female problems." This type of problem is completely beyond most men's grasp, but when your wife is acting a little bit loopy you need some type of title for their behavior. "Female problems" just has a good ring to it and it covers about everything. As he walked into the kitchen, Lori was stacking plates and bowls on the kitchen table. Without being asked, she answered, "I saw a few bugs and I'm going to put a bug bomb off as we go to work tomorrow". "OK then," Gene said, "I'm going to head on to bed 'cause I've got a full day tomorrow and I need my beauty sleep."

The next morning, the alarm went off at 5:15. As he came back into the bedroom, he noticed that Lori wasn't up moving around yet. He went back to the bedroom to check on her. She sleepily said she was going to call in to the office and maybe go in later. Her head had been hurting all night. Gene said he hoped she felt better and headed on to work. If he was going to be on time, he needed to go because the Jacksonville highway system could be very unforgiving if you were even a few minutes off your routine.

The afternoon seemed pretty uneventful. As he pulled into the driveway, he noticed that one of the trash cans had been run over. He made a mental note to tell that trash man a thing or two about respecting his property the next time he saw him.

He walked in and knew almost immediately that something was amiss. The house just felt cold, but not in the cool type of way. He took his work boots off at the kitchen table and sat them next to the door leading out to the car port. As he turned around, he saw the note.

Gene,
"I love and care about you,
But, I'm not in love with you anymore
I want a family and you can't give me one
I'm going to find it, Please don't try to find me..."

Lori

Gene's whole world went black at that moment. Maybe life was just too much for him. Nothing had gone smoothly since he couldn't remember when. How could this be happening? How could she just walk away like this? What about all of their plans? What about the house? Jesus Christ, what was he supposed to do now? Where was he supposed to go now?

He walked into the living room and looked around. Not much was gone. He walked into their bedroom and looked into her closet. It was true. She had taken her clothes. His wife had left him. He looked at the bed that she had made for the last time and began the process of falling completely apart. He would sit alone in the living room for the next two days. It was hard at that time to discern what was real and what wasn't. In the back of his mind, he hoped that she would have a change of heart and return home, but he knew that would never happen. Somewhere in this relationship he hadn't taken the time to care for her personal needs and he was paying for it with every beat of his heart. He had, of course, explained to her that he couldn't give her children before she married him, but at the time, she hadn't seemed to care. He wondered if he had only given more of himself to her, if he had been there for her more often, would she still be here? But at the same time, she had always been the type of women that not only wanted, but needed her personal space. His mind was in a spin and he didn't know how to get it back on track. He had felt the pain of a broken body and all of the future pain that the plane crash would bring, but he had never felt pain like this in his life. As a matter of fact, he didn't even know this type of pain even existed.

The phone rang, but he didn't hear it. Someone knocked on the side door and then tried the front doorbell. Again, Gene didn't hear anything. His world was lost. He had allowed himself, along with his spirit, to walk away without ever leaving the house. It would be twenty two days before friends and family became worried enough to get a key to his house and go inside and check on him. Melissa called her aunt, Gene's sister, and she stopped by on a rainy morning to find her brother an unshaven, disheveled mess. Phone calls were made to family members, but no one knew what to do to help him. They didn't believe he was thinking or acting rationally. He might even be suicidal. More phone calls were made to some local facilities that dealt with mental trauma. Melissa found out that the state of Florida had a law in place for situations not unlike this called the "Baker Act." This law allowed any three family members to have a loved one committed for seventy two hours to ensure their safety and be certain that no harm would come to them.

Melissa called the police and asked them to take Gene to the hospital for observation. But when they arrived, Gene told them the story about his wife and convinced them that he was not suicidal.

He just needed to get back to work and have time to process what had happened to him and his marriage. The following morning, Gene did make it to work, but it was a useless attempt. He hadn't realized it at the time, but his heart, body and mind were off-kilter. He had just had more than his mind could handle. So many traumatic things had happened without any time for Gene to deal with the mental anguish. This was the final straw for Gene Odom and it would be a while before he would find true clarity.

Chapter 18
June 1989

"Take the air that I breathe, close the door when you leave"

AFTER BEING CLOSELY OBSERVED BY a doctor and his staff in Lake City, Gene was released. The general consensus was that he had bounced back from his loss and was prepared to get on with his life. Upon getting back home, Gene needed to return to work because he had gone several weeks without any income or making payments to his debtors. Things went smoothly for the first few days, but there was no denying the shadow cast by the large Blue Cross building in downtown Jacksonville. Every time Gene looked to the east of the building he was working on, he saw the large structure with the dark blue glass windows that had once been the workplace of the woman he loved. One afternoon, Gene went to the corner hot dog stand for lunch. While standing in line, he spoke to one of his ex-wife's co-workers. She casually mentioned that she was down the hall from someone that spoke to Lori on a daily basis on the inner office phone system. What the lady failed to mention and probably didn't know was that Lori was indeed working for

Blue Cross again, just not in Jacksonville. She was in fact, more than four hundred miles away at a Virginia branch office.

This tidbit of misinformation hit Gene like a bolt of lightning, and he lost all rational thought. He left work, drove to a friends' house, and got an antique pistol. After putting the pistol in the passenger seat of the car, he drove back to the Blue Cross parking garage. Gene gave the guard in the guard shack a note telling him to send his wife to the top level of the parking structure and that he wasn't leaving until he spoke to her. The guard had seen the pistol in the seat beside Gene, had seen the confusion in Gene's eyes, and had also read the note given to him. The police were called, and the police called the SWAT team in case a turn of events caused the situation to get out of hand.

Gene sat out in the sun, baking in his blue1973 Chevrolet Impala. As the sweat got in his eyes he would close them for a moment, but all he could see was Lori. This day was probably not going to end well. He needed to tell her how he felt about her. She needed to understand what she had done. What she had caused. He didn't notice the men in the blue helmets and sunglasses getting into position with rifles pointing towards his heart. He didn't care anyway. Some members of the elite team slowly came up the side exit stairs and asked Gene if he would consider talking to them. Gene told them to go away. He was there to talk things over with his wife and wasn't leaving until she came out and settled this once and for all. Hours went by. The heat was nearly unbearable. A few hundred feet away, a small robot was cruising in Gene's direction. The small device pulled up alongside his car and sat silently with a telephone for him to use just in case he decided he needed to talk to someone. Sweat continued to pour out of his body. The rifles and their scopes continued to point directly at his heart from three spots above the garage. In his peripheral vision, Gene noticed a bottle of orange Gatorade sitting in the back seat. He reached back, got the bottle, and began to drink. Within a few more minutes a man with a speaker instructed Gene to pick up the phone. During these moments the drink seemed to allow his dehydrated mind to think a little bit more clearly than it had been. When he picked up the phone, he was greeted from the other end with a gentle, calming voice. The man told Gene that he didn't want the afternoon to end badly, but they had to come to some type of agreement. The offices would be closing within the hour, he said, and he couldn't allow a man with a gun to be endangering the employees. Gene told the officer that he didn't have any idea what was going on. "I'm extremely ill. How can I put an end to this?" He was instructed to get out of the car very slowly, leave the gun in his car, and lay face down on the pavement with his hands on his head. He was told that they would be taking charge of the situation.

Gene was transported to a command vehicle where he was allowed to speak to Lori. She told him to stay with those men. They were going to get him the help that he needed, and she would see him soon.

*With dehydration, particularly an acute situation like sitting in that car, what happens is the extracellular fluid (fluid outside the cells) becomes depleted, creating a relative increase in the sodium concentration in the blood extracellular space. To compensate for this, the intracellular fluid (the fluid inside of our cells) is pulled out by the ion gradient created by the relative increase in extracellular sodium concentration. When that happens, the cells begin to shrink because all of the fluid is being pulled out. This has a dramatic effect on our brain cells and can cause profound confusion, delirium, loss of consciousness and finally death as the cells cease to function. As well, the dehydration causes acute renal failure (which is reversible with hydration), but this typically causes muscle- ache type symptoms.

In Gene's case, the swat team incident was preceded by that extended period of time where he didn't likely eat or drink much during those twenty-two days he was alone in his house. This likely left him in a catabolic state of breaking down a lot of protein and muscle mass to survive, which also takes a toll on the kidneys and electrolyte balance, as well as causing lactic acidosis. Because of the entire ordeal, he probably had a very low threshold for dehydration, along with post- traumatic stress that could have easily lent itself to a psychotic break. He theoretically could have experienced significant confusion in a relatively short period of time.

Chapter 19
1989-1990

"You Tore My World Apart"

A S GENE SAT IN THE empty hospital room, his confusion turned to disdain for the emotions that he had felt. A warm, inviting home had been traded in for a concrete masonry structure with cold fluorescent lights and a hard bed. He had even lost the most basic privacies. The bathroom had been locked, there were no windows giving daylight, and he was being watched like a zoo animal. The time that had been invested along with the faith that he had had in Lori had been betrayed. He had lost twenty -seven pounds in twenty-one days. His body was weak, his mind was void of all rational thought, and, as far as he was concerned, the end for everyone even remotely involved in this fiasco was very near.

As the first days passed, once again he was faced with the realization that Lori had told him yet another lie. She had not called like she promised. The dark clouds of hatred began to work their awful magic. He was planning to escape the facility, find Lori and take her life. Logic had left the building.

Because of Gene's situation, everything that he did was closely monitored. Food, exercise, and medication were given on a stiff daily regimen. Unfortunately, the staff hadn't taken enough precaution as far as his medication was concerned. He wasn't taking it. He had been hiding it under his tongue and getting rid of the medicine as he was given the opportunity. He was eating though. He was also exercising regularly. If he was going to kill his wife and any unlucky soul that stood in his way, he was going to need his strength.

The desk that monitored all of the patients in Gene's area was just down the hall from his room. He would go there to receive his daily medication, counseling schedule, basic toiletries, and anything else that he needed. It was during one of these visits that Gene noticed one of the orderlies taking a patient outside to get some sun. The exit door did not completely shut and lock. He went down the hall to a call a friend on the pay phone. Gene told his friend that he would be on the corner of Beach Boulevard and University Boulevard and to please come and pick him up quickly.

Gene went to his room and got what few items he had together and proceeded to walk right out the door. Upon walking out of the building, he was immediately noticed by the male orderly. The orderly calmly spoke to Gene, reminding him that he was not allowed to be outside alone yet and gently touched Gene's arm. Gene positioned his body in such a way that he could hit the man with a punch to the side of the head knocking the man out cold. He looked at the seven- foot wrought iron fence, took off running towards it and easily was on the other side of it in seconds. Immediately, guards and nurses were everywhere trying to catch up. Gene ran down the road only to realize that his first choice of direction was leading to a dead end. Seconds later, he could see the red lights coming in his direction. Gene decided it best to just sit down on a bench and wait for his ride back to the facility. Upon being returned, he was asked the obvious question: "Why did you leave?" Gene told his doctor that he just needed some air and that he did not feel like he deserved to be confined since, as far as they knew, he had done everything that had been asked of him. After listening to and believing his story, the doctor said he would be allowed more freedom if he would give his word that he would make no more attempts to leave. Gene agreed.

For the following month, Gene spent his time exercising and eating as healthily as possible. In his mind, he felt it important that he was in as good physical shape as possible if he were to be successful at killing his wife.

As time passed, Gene seemed like he was settling back into sanity. He was allowed to return home. He went back to work and began focusing on getting his bills caught back up. Somehow, his previous plan of murder had diminished. He resigned himself to attempting to speak with Lori. This wasn't to be, either. His wife was terrified of him and rightly so. He did, however, have the opportunity to meet with her mother. He told his side of the story, she politely listened, and he went home realizing that it was time to get on with his life and she would need to be given the opportunity to live hers.

Chapter 20
1990

"Love letters from the Edge of Middle-Aged crazy"

GENE ADAPTED TO SANITY QUICKLY. He began working as an ironworker at the Bush Brewery and moved out on Collins road onto five rural acres just outside of Jacksonville. He spent the better part of the next year working and creek fishing. Being alone gave him the time to heal and get caught up on his bills.

Gene would once again experience his fatefully bad luck on September 12, 1990. While working, he fell about twenty feet off of some steel that he had been working on. His liver was badly damaged, and it was determined that he had probably fallen due to pre- existing nerve and spinal damage from the plane crash. There would be no more construction work for Gene. He was placed on disability and he would again need to look for a new direction with his life.

Almost like clockwork, the phone rang one evening. On the other end was his lifelong friend Johnny Van Zant, Ronnie's little brother. Johnny had just released his Brickyard Road single and was getting ready to go out on the road in support of the album. He was going to be opening for ZZ Top and asked Gene if he would like to travel with them and sell his book and other merchandise. This would be a great opportunity for Gene to get out of the house and allow him to get back on the road for a while. Things went well for Johnny and, in turn, things went well for Gene. The tour lasted for about five months.

During one of the many shows across the countryside, Gene met a young lady named Terri Sue. She must have been quite smitten by Gene, because she found herself moving about one thousand miles south of her hometown and into the swamps with him. She adapted quickly to her new surroundings and found a job at the very facility Gene had been removed from by the SWAT team not so long before. Blue Cross Blue Shield offered her a great job with excellent benefits, and along with its' irony, it seemed like a good fit. Terri Sue didn't end up "adapting" as well as one would think, though. She didn't like the heat, she didn't like what the humidity did to her hair, and when she was about to start her menstrual cycle, she didn't like Gene all that much either. Gene began to feel like a ghost in his own home. He would come home only to find this young women looking right through him. Gene felt like whatever "shine" the young girl thought he had, he had obviously lost it and it was time for her to move back to the Midwest and have a big litter of ugly, little kids. Terri Sue moved out exactly one year to the day from when she moved in. Florida isn't for everybody. And that is probably a good thing if you have ever experienced snowbird traffic.

Later that same year, Gene passed a Jeep that had broken down alongside the road. Having plenty of time on his hands, he stopped to help the unfortunate driver out. As luck would have it, the driver was actually a girl from Gene's junior high school named Jane. He got the Jeep running, laughed about the irony, and exchanged phone numbers with her. They began dating and seemed to get along quite well. Months passed, and she invited him to move into the house that she shared with her sister and daughter. Gene felt like maybe his luck had finally changed. They seemed to all get along great, the little girl truly enjoyed his being around, and he enjoyed her as well. The next few years would be a welcome break from all of the unneeded drama that he had been forced to endure.

Unfortunately, towards the end of the second year, he would find out that Jane was having an affair with a young man half her age. He confronted her with the ugly facts, and she, in turn, denied everything accusing him of being a "crazy redneck." Gene felt like it would be best to move out to avoid any unnecessary conflict around the young daughter. Mr. Leonard Skinner had a guest house behind his home that Gene moved into. Gene was still committed to the relationship with Jane though and was hoping that this storm would pass. While he was mowing her grass one afternoon he went inside to call his doctor about an afternoon appointment. Beside the phone sat a small envelope with the name of the young man who had been seeing Jane on it. Gene didn't feel right about going through someone else's mail but he knew without a shadow of a doubt that this was indeed the smoking gun that he needed to finally find out where he stood with this woman. Sure enough, it was a "love letter" from a fifty- year- old woman to a twenty- five-year- old kid. A few days would pass before Jane appeared at Gene's house asking for forgiveness. She was instructed in no uncertain terms to get her big butt out of his house and out of the yard.

Apparently, that was Gene's last attempt at love with a woman. He has told me that he doesn't have the money or the trust required to ever consider or be considered by another woman. I hope that this policy doesn't stay in place. He has much to offer, and if you happen to be a lonely woman with a lot of money that likes to fish, hates cats, and would consider buying a nice boat, call me and I'll give you his number. I may require a finders fee.

Chapter 21
1992-2009

"Forever Theirs"

Coach Leonard Skinner had enjoyed being the namesake for the Skynyrd band. Because of his famous name, as well as an apparent business savvy, he had owned a successful real estate company and a string of southern rock bars bearing his name. All the while, he and Gene had remained close friends.

Gene had recently moved into the guest house of the Skinner estate. Unfortunately, Mr. Skinner and his wife realized not long after Gene moved into the guest house that their home was too big now that their kids were grown up. They would be putting their house on the market, and Gene would again need to find a place to live. Gene had a boyhood friend named John Ferrell that mentioned that his dad was alone in a big house and would appreciate Gene's company. John's father was already sick with lung cancer, and Gene took him to his treatments until he passed away. Tom and John Ferrell have both spoken with me about that period in their lives as they watched helplessly while the cancer took their father from them. They have found great comfort in knowing that Gene was there for their dad around the clock offering encouragement and comfort to the father as well as the sons. A local doctor that knew Gene mentioned that he wanted to sell his hunting cabin that sat on the Withlacoochee River in Inverness Florida. Within a week, Gene was living in the swamp, sharing his immediate area with nine alligators and more raccoons than he could count. Life was very good and those starry Florida nights were even better. After so many years of pushing, it was nice to finally reflect on the life that had been handed to him. The final analysis of Gene's health had been delivered. He had hoped to work at least in some limited capacity, but Gene would not be allowed to work any job of any kind for the rest of his life. I am sure that this was very hard for a man like Gene to swallow. But he was determined to carry on.

Gene's daughter Melissa announced that she was going to be married and was hoping to have that perfect wedding that all girls dream about. Gene told his little girl to put the wedding together and send him the bill.

The big day arrived and she was as beautiful as any princess in any storybook. Her wedding was everything she had ever dreamed about. No one knew until after the fact that Gene had sold his house and used the profit to pay for the wedding. He still had his G.I. Bill to fall back on and found a home built in 1978 for $55,000. Gene went to work updating the place at his own pace until it was the perfect home for a single gentleman. After about one year, the phone rang with the news that would break his heart. His three year old grandson was sick with leukemia in Oklahoma. Gene was out the door headed up the highway to see what he could do, how he could help. Upon arrival, it didn't take long to see that the little family was overburdened. They had five little children, and it took two cars just to move the family at one time. Due to the recent medical bills, they were also suffering financially. After a week, Gene headed back to Florida. He knew his grandson was going to have a rough road ahead, and he would need both parents in the same car at the very least. The Inverness Florida Chrysler dealership had just put the new 2005 mini vans on the lot when Gene drove by. He stopped, considered his daughter's family's situation, and bought a van. Once again, he had to sell his home to make this purchase, but he didn't even blink. The newly updated home sold before Gene could deliver the van to Oklahoma. Gene delivered the title and the keys and took a plane back to Florida. When he got back home there was already a family moving into his house. He picked up his boxes, took them to a storage facility, found his fishing pole, and went to the riverbank so he could think.

Today, Gene is living with his oldest daughter Melissa, her husband David, their little boy Colby, and their little girl Chesney Jean. Gene described himself as a sixty- year- old- man that shovels dog crap in the backyard and is on disability. That is not how I would describe him at all. I see a man that loves his friends and family. I see a man that has a big story to tell with an endless supply of life lessons. Tonight when you look in the mirror, ask yourself if you would put your life on the line for your best friend. Could you keep it together when trouble just keeps on knocking at your door? Would you give up everything to care for your children? There is a lot more about Gene Odom and Lynyrd Skynyrd that I haven't told you. I can assure you of one thing though. He was there for Ronnie Van Zant on that plane, trying to save his friend until all hope was lost in that Mississippi swamp. He was there for Gary and Allen too, as well as Ronnie's widow, Judy, during the aftermath of the crash. He has obviously made mistakes, but his love is pure for his daughters and their mother, as well as his grandchildren. I feel honored just to know him and call him my friend. I know firsthand why he was Ronnie's best friend. I also know why he is one of mine.

Gene and I have driven the neighborhood where he spent his childhood, we have stood outside of the house that he and his second wife shared before she walked away, and we have walked together through the cemetery where Ronnie Van Zant, Ronnie's parents, Leon Wilkeson, and Allen Collins and his wife and baby are buried. I have read about the "so-called" curse of Skynyrd. I have endured stories of Ronnie supposedly knowing he wouldn't live to be thirty years old. I have even read an article about people insisting that they have witnessed Ronnie's ghost at the bank of his favorite fishing hole. I am not an expert in any of these fields, especially ghost chasing. (Truth be told, I'm not an expert at anything.) The media feels the need to tell stories that don't need to be told and they will write and sensationalize nearly anything to sell a magazine or a book.

Chapter 22
2010

"Considering Gene and Ronnie's Friendship"

LIKE I SAID WHEN I started this book, I wasn't sure what the final outcome was going to be. Sure, I had aspirations of unearthing a raw talent in myself that hadn't been seen since Hemingway or Steinbeck or Salinger. Well, we both know that didn't happen. What did I find? Honestly, I'm still in the process of clarifying it myself. On the one hand, I see a simple man that has experienced some pretty terrible things and walked away from it with his integrity and natural- born love for his friends and family without bitterness and resentment. So many people have pulled him this way and that wanting to know more about Ronnie, their friendship, the band, and of course the crash. I have spent many hours with Gene. We have talked, and I have listened to the stories about his and Ronnie's friendship. I have heard things about the band I hate to believe. But at the end of the day, they still walk on water as far as I'm concerned. And the plane crash? Good Lord, that is and was a true nightmare.

I wanted to take you with me on the rest of this ride and talk about some of the facts. Where do we start? Both Gene and Ronnie grew up in a rough little area like millions of other American kids did and still do. They both loved the basic things that all little kids love like sports, soda, and plenty of sunshine. Gene, the man, is a realist. He wanted nothing more than the American dream. A wife, a few kids, a good job, and house would have made him happy. Ronnie, on the other hand was a dreamer, with a serious drive. Let's face it. He wasn't a great singer. He was a good singer. He wasn't tall, dark, and handsome. He was short and stocky and about to lose his hair. The real difference in Ronnie from others was his desire to rise above normalcy. That is not to say that he wasn't a normal guy. According to Gene, he was absolutely the most down- to- earth guy you could have ever met. He was the kind of man that you would have liked to sit down on a porch with, share jokes with, and talk about what's going on in your lives. Ronnie Van Zant was a visionary. When he was young kid, he had plans of being a famous boxer. Then a famous race car driver, and finally the leader of a rock 'n' roll band after seeing the Rolling Stones. Do you see the pattern here? In the midst of all of these dreams his friendship with Gene always lasted. When Ronnie came home off the road Gene would be one of his first stops. They just liked hanging out. I think that Ronnie respected Gene because he stood firm in his own beliefs without judging others. Gene made the decision early on not to drink, smoke, or do drugs. But even though Ronnie did all of the above to an extreme, he and Gene were pals.

Gene has told me that Ronnie just wanted to have nice things. He didn't have to have the flashy things. His bass boat wasn't anything special, but it floated and did the job it was intended to do. Ronnie put "Bad Company" decals on the side of the boat because that was his favorite band. Ronnie never had a mansion. He had a ranch house out on Brickyard Road in Orange Park facing Doctor's Lake. Just before he died, he and his wife Judy, were thinking about moving into a subdivision so their little girl Melody would have other kids to play with instead of alligators, cottonmouths, and raccoons. He had a Jeep, liked old pick-up trucks and Merle Haggard, Tom T. Hall and George Jones.

Gene has told me that he has absolutely no doubt in his mind that Ronnie would have quit the drugs and alcohol. He wasn't happy with his situation and was in the process of making some big changes. The others in the band would have had to straighten up as well because Ronnie would have demanded it. I was very happy to hear this. The lyrics in those songs never did sound like words written by an addict; they sounded like words from a solid-thinking man with ideas. Ronnie had good ideas.

Ronnie was very proud of his family. He loved his brothers and sisters very much. He also thought the world of his parents. What else can I tell you? Ronnie was a good person, and I understand fully now why he and Gene were so tight and why Ronnie thought so much of Gene. Someone told me that the closest distance between two friends is laughter. Gene and Ronnie had a lot of laughs and it seems like every time I talk to Gene these days, we still take time to laugh.

But there is something else worth mentioning. I have spoken to several good people while gathering information on Gene Odom. Truth be told, all of these people have a story that should be heard. Like I mentioned at the very beginning of the book, Gene Odom is part of the fabric that has made our country great. All of these people must be cut from the same cloth. I have spoken to hardworking, honest people. The kind of people we all wish we knew more of. Ronnie Van Zant and Lee Roy Yarborough made a name for themselves, no question about it. A big name isn't the only thing that makes people great, though. I hope to keep all of these people in my life. I appreciate what they did to help me and Gene put this book together. If possible, it would just be good to know there are more Americans like the ones from the west side of Jacksonville, Florida.

I have talked to Gene about the aging process. As I look at Gene and think about all that he has shared with me about his life, it begins to dawn on me that what I want most for you is to know him the way that I know him. I want you, the reader, to see what an interesting and good individual this guy really is. In my mind I do not equate him with the band. He wasn't part of the band. He was there friend. It is a shame to me that over the last thirty years or so Gene and Gary Rossington don't talk any more. Some silly stuff from too long ago has gotten in the way of friendship and that is sad. I had hoped that they could get together and talk things through. Gene could sure use Gary's help these days, but he would never dream of asking for it. I tend to think boyhood friends that survive a freaking plane crash would find a way to work out a few issues, but I'm sure I am not qualified to be their judge.

It seems like most of our problems always stem with something to do with money and this time was no different. Gene had gone to court to testify on behalf of Ronnie's wife, Judy to ensure that she would maintain some status as shareholder in the new line-up of Lynyrd Skynyrd. This happened following the 1987-1988 tours. Prior to this, on April 13, 1983, Gene had a letter signed by Allen, Gary, Billy, and Leon, as well Artimus, and Teresa Gains who were not original shareholders. As a result of Gene's testimony and a signed piece of paper, Judy Van Zant was allowed to share in the proceeds of all concert money's. The end result however, would be the loss of a lifelong friend in Gary Rossington.

In Closing

I WAS ABOUT FIFTEEN YEARS old when it first hit me. I had grown up listening to a wide range of country music, occasionally drifting off into some of the music my oldest sister had in her car. I happened to hear some kids in high school playing "Free Bird" at a school talent contest, and it blew my mind. I was in town that week at Val's Discount store purchasing "One More from the Road" and never really looked back. (I thought Gary Rossington, Allen Collins, and Ed King were the coolest guitar players ever and I still do.) As I have said earlier, I still listen to a massive amount of music, but nothing runs as deep with me as Lynyrd Skynyrd. I have never had the tendency to lift people too high off the ground. I appreciate what people do, but it is important not to have idols. Idols will ultimately disappoint us. I believe the songs are the important part.

During some of the interviews preparing for this book, I have been told true, unadulterated stories that I chose not to include. Many of those stories I wish I had never heard. Some time ago, I had the opportunity to sit down with Charlie Daniels. He and I had time to talk a little about Ronnie and their friendship. He told me that Ronnie was at a crossroads when the "Street Survivors" album was being recorded. He agrees that given time Ronnie would have made the right decision about his lifestyle, but unfortunately the plane crash took that decision off the table. Always remember one thing, though. Gene Odom was right there with Ronnie, trying to help him and his friends before he helped himself. He was doing exactly what he was hired to do, all the way to the ground. Tom Ferrell called me from Jacksonville one Sunday evening as I was near completion of this book. He grew up around Gene. (You may remember Gene living with Tom's father earlier in the book.) Tom, like so many others, offered nothing but kind words concerning Gene. These days, Mr. Odom doesn't have a lot of the material "extras". He's given everything to take care of his family. Gene does have however, excessive amounts of integrity, loyalty to friends and family, and love and respect returned to him. Tom told me stories of the "old days" when Gene was more of a big brother figure to him. When people have talked to me about Gene, the one thing they keep coming back to is the consistency of his goodness. Don't get me wrong, I'm not trying to turn him into a saint. But if you have read this book, you must agree that he has seen hard times and proven to be, at the very least resilient.

I was hoping that there would be a series of life lessons in this book. I wanted the reader to know all about the life of Gene Odom. I want all of you to know about his thoughts and feelings. I figured at the very least I'd just go on the road with a power-point and amaze everyone with my remarkable insight into restructuring the plight of mankind. (I don't see that happening any time soon.) I do hope you found the book interesting. I hope you realize that I tried my best not to slight anyone mentioned.

Gene has told me that his hope was that this book would somehow release him from the 1977 tragedy. That was over thirty years ago. We shouldn't have to be defined by a single moment in our lives. He and I decided early on that his story is an interesting one, and continues to this very day. He has come a long way from that little boy picking up soda bottles…I'm very glad he and I are such close friends...I'm glad that the music led me to him. Curtis Loew, indeed...

Some of Gene's Poetry:

Naturally

Don't try to make me something
That I'm not meant to be
Don't ask me to smile for a camera
That I can't see
Don't push things at me
That you're hung up on
There's places in this life that I stand alone
I cannot be anything that I am not
Naturally

Days Long Gone

It's the same old story
Everywhere I go
They see my eyes
And my scars
But what do they really want to know?
I am chained to the past
But wanting to travel on
With memories still present
Of days long gone

My Old Fishing Buddy

I loved you when you was down and out
I loved you when you was a star
Oh yes I still love you friend
I just can't see where you are
Do you like being an Angel?
This I've got to know
My old fishing buddy
Of not so long ago
Remember our favorite creek
The one so dark and muddy
I'll always remember you both
My ole' fishing buddy

Ronnie's Song

I was asleep in my bed in the middle of the night
When I awoke in a cold sweat
I was dreaming of a happening
A time in the past
When I saw some friends of mine in a distant place
Was this a dream I was dreaming?
Was this a vision that I had seen?
He told me to tell the boys to keep on playing
Because there is more of the song to sing
I saw a barefoot shadow walking toward me
Wearing a black hat and a black shirt
He spoke to me and I was in a daze
"Listen to me, friend, I've got something to say."
We talked for a while
Then he said, "I'll be seeing you.
Take care of my boys friend, you know what to do."
Was this a dream I was dreaming?
Was this a vision that I had seen?
He told me to tell the boys to keep playing
Because there is more of the song to sing
Tell everybody I love them
Especially my family
Tell them I'll always be around
Because I'm part of that old southern town
Pray for me and think of me
Let my name be a household sound
I'm not that far away, just in another town
Thunder and lightening began to roar
Drums and guitars began to soar
A voice I've always known and loved
Cried out from the heavens above
Keep on playing and one day

We'll all be free
He turned and walked away
Right out of my sight
Like a shadow would do
In the darkest of night

Gene Odom (1980)

Acknowledgments:

FINALLY, IT HAS BEEN TWO years now since I started this book. With work and family as well as other happenings, it took a lot longer than I originally anticipated. It is funny how something like this has allowed me to better understand myself. What I originally planned for this project hasn't exactly transpired, but I am happy with the end result because I think the book will serve its purpose.

I appreciate my wife, Cynthia, being so supportive during the writing process. We had to spend money we really didn't have in our budget to allow me to travel to meet different people from Gene's past as well as many other unexpected costs.

I want to thank Joel Beavins and his wife Dr. Jill Beavins for the valuable information on the plane wreck as well as allowing for understandable explanations for some of Gene's physical problems that he has had to endure.

Thank you to my little cousin Nancy Coner for editing this book. If there is anything wrong, and I know there is, it is totally my fault. She did an outstanding job.

I hope that all of the nice people that I have met and interviewed know how much I have appreciated them as well as their valuable time. I love those old photographs.

Emily Coner

I also wanted to thank my daughter Emily for doing such a nice job on the book cover. She is fifteen years old with an outstanding future ahead of her.

Gene, I hope this book is something that you can be proud of. Thank you for being my friend.

Joseph Scott Coner (2011)

A letter from Gene Odom:

"I WAS SITTING IN THE swing with the dog on a hot Sunday afternoon when I got a call from Billy Webb. He said a feller E-mailed him on the web site and he wanted to meet with me. This guy's name was Scott Coner and he had a friend that was real sick with cancer that wanted to visit where Skynyrd and I come from. I said sure, come on down and I'll show y'all a good time.

Well, we went all over Jacksonville having a good ole' time. We went to the old neighborhood where me and Ronnie and the rest of the boys grew up, we went to the swamp to visit the old hell house, we visited The Jug, then we visited the grave sites.

During the evenings me and Scott got to talking about my life. I had mentioned to him that a lot had taken place since that plane crash. I guess to be honest with you, my life hasn't been a graceful one. I suppose I've muddled through. I've got my daughters and my grandkids and I think that that is all that matters anymore to me anyway.

I appreciate Scott taking the time to let me ramble on about my life, my history, and the way it all ended up. Looking back over all of it now, I wish I could change some things. I've sure known some good women, had some good friends, and lost a few of both. My old buddy Ronnie would have sure liked Scott. They both have lots of talent and to tell the truth, Scott reminds me of him in a lot of ways. I think we did a good job with my life and Scott's words.

103

I would like to thank all of the people that had stories and pictures for this little book. Some of them brought back a flood of memories. I will probably forget some people, but that can be expected I guess with a mind this old and battered. My two ex-wives Lori and Brenda had pictures and memories that dang near put my good eye out. My two daughters, Mellisa Jean and Christina Diane came up with some stuff that I had tried to forget about. Thanks girls. My oldest sister Vivian had stuff I ain't seen since the fifties. This was like going back in time and having trouble leaving. Another sister Joyce came up with some stuff as well and I really do appreciate it. My old friends Pete, Randy, John and Tom Ferrell, and Bill Hodge had stories I guess I had forgotten about.

My buddy Billy Webb found a couple of guys, Ben Upham and Brandon Campbell, that had some old Skynyrd pictures from the seventies that were really something else. These pictures show an old friends desire to make it to the top. He made it and he ain't come down yet. Like I said already, my friend Scott Coner did a great job and I can't thank him enough. I hope you enjoy the book.

Thanks,
Gene

CPSIA information can be obtained
at www.ICGtesting.com
Printed in the USA
BVHW040227170323
660516BV00004B/566